THE

WICKED

SHALL

RISE NO MORE

TELLA OLAYERI

+2348023583168

Published By:

GOD'S LINK VENTURES

Email tellaolayeri@gmail.com

Website www.tellaolayeri.com

US Contact
Ruth Jack
14 Milewood Road
Verbank
N.Y.12585
U.S.A. +19176428989

DEDICATION

This book is dedicated to the **HOLY GHOST** for inspiring me to write this eye opening book.

APPRECIATION

My appreciation goes to my dedicated wife, **MRS NGOZI OLAYERI,** who typed the manuscript of this book and designed the cover page. My darling wife I say thank you. My appreciation equally goes to my lovely children, **MISS IBUKUN, DAVID, MICHAEL COMFORT and MERCY.** They encouraged me day and night as I write this book

Respect and honor should be given to who is due. Favor comes from God and men as well. My calling (writing evangelism) met the timely support of a particular man of God, preacher, teacher, prophet and General Overseer. He awakes my inner man and gave me sound spiritual support. Without his earlier support for my first book, *Fire for Fire Prayer Book* and subsequent ones, I may not be where I am today in Christian literature writing. He gallantly stood by me in fulfillment of my calling.

This book you are holding is a testimony of my claim. This book wouldn't have seen the light of the day, if not for the spiritual encouragement I gathered from my father in the Lord who served as spiritual mirror that brightens my hope to explore my calling.

I am talking of no any other person than the **General Overseer of MOUNTAIN OF FIRE**

AND MIRACLES MINISTRIES WORLD WIDE, DR. D. K. OLUKOYA.

Once again, I say thank you sir. Your support has yielded yet another earth shaking book.
THANKS
Evangelist Tella Olayeri.

PREFACE

This book is a great revealer of how the wicked operates and destroy destiny of people. Those that operate under the cover of witchcraft are wicked and merciless. No one wish the wicked well as they attack foundation and career of people. These enemies of progress hate peace, but confusion and agony in the life of others.

This book reveals how wicked and heartless the wicked are. Their curriculum is evil, what they know is evil, what they do is evil, their food is evil, so is their expectation. The book tells us, no one come across them and smile. It is always sorrow, tears and blood. The wicked shall rise no more is the language, the righteous says in heaven, even here on earth.

It is time you wake from slumber and pray every prayer in this book. It is you that will announce the obituary of your enemy and not, other way round. The time is now; there should be no further delay. As soldiers of Christ, put on the whole armor of God and see wonders of God. There is no time God is happy with the wicked. God doesn't want the righteous to be in agony, he wants them equipped and courageous to face and demolish the works of darkness. He knows the wicked are witches and wizards that don't want you to rise. He is waiting for you to pray and be delivered. I pray you shall be delivered from the oppression of the wicked today, in the name of Jesus.

This book is loaded with Holy Spirit vomited prayer that shakes the foundation of the wicked, scatter them and destroy them in numbers. At the end, the enemy that pursues you shall fall and rise no more. The one that rob and held to your possession in the spirit shall surrender them, and rise no more. The one that rob your career shall release it by fire. Those that gather against you day and night shall woefully fail.

It is time you rise and shine. It is time you witness the obituary of the enemy that boast he shall not let you go and do well in life. It is time to be victorious and occupy your mountain top. The day is today, no power shall rob you of it.

I say congratulation as you walk into a new dawn. The Lord Almighty shall bless you; your mouth shall be filled with laughter and joy. Amen.

GOOD NEWS!!!

My audiobook is now available, to get one visit **acx.com** and search **"Tella Olayeri."**

Brethren, to be loaded and reloaded visit: *amazon.com/author/tellaolayeri* for a full spiritual sojourn for my books.

Thanks.

PREVIOUS PUBLICATIONS OF THE AUTHOR

1. 100% CONFESSIONS and PROPHECIES to Locate Helpers and helpers to locate you
2. 1000 Prayer Points for Children Breakthrough
3. 1010 (One Thousand and Ten) DREAMS and Interpretations
4. 2000 Dangerous Prayer for First Born
5. 365 DREAMS and INTERPRETATIONS
6. 430 Prayers to Cancel Bad Dreams and Overcome Witchcraft Powers part one (DREAMS AND YOU Book 1)
7. 430 Prayers to Claim Good Dreams and Overcome Witchcraft Powers part two (DREAMS AND YOU Book 2)
8. 630 Acidic Prayers: With Missile Prayer for Speedy Breakthrough, Healing and Deliverance
9. 650 DREAMS AND INTERPRETATIONS
10. 700 Prayers to Clear Unemployment Out of Your Way
11. 720 Missile Prayers that Silence Enemies: Prayers that Bring Peace and Rest
12. 740 Rocket Prayers that Break Satanic Embargo
13. 777 Deliverance Prayers for Healing and Breakthrough
14. 800 Deliverance Prayer for Middle Born: Daily Devotional for Teen and Adult

See all at: <u>amazon.com/author/tellaolayeri</u>

Table of Contents

CHAPTER 1

THE WICKED SHALL RISE NO MORE

Everyone have good vision to fulfill in life. In the beginning, God says we shall have dominion over all his creation. Power of dominion is with us but we refuse to dominate, because of our sin, unrighteousness and the wickedness of our heart. The wicked change the course of our destiny and make things difficult for us to bear.

The question is, who are the wicked? They are evil doers whose life is full of sin. They commit evil at free will. Wickedness is synonym to sin. The wicked are criminals in the spirit and in the physical. Wickedness is a mental disregard for justice. The wicked reduce virtue of men and women to nothing. Being wicked sometimes, brought God's curse upon us. Thoughts of men to each other are full of wickedness; hardly a day goes by without thought of wickedness in our heart to our neighbor, family, race or nation. It is God and God only that can separate wickedness from our heart.

You have one excuse or the other against someone. You want to revenge of the past because you have un-forgiven spirit. You hate a tribe, a race either, black, colored or white, all these are wickedness. We think of others wickedness, but often forget our thought against friends, neighbors or enemies. You must pray to God, and wash your heart clean of evil thought and be righteous. Try and avoid trouble so that your heart may be clean and close to God. Try to forgive and forget, no matter how difficult. If you are seriously hurt, pray to God to help you out.

But then, you must go into battle in prayer and take serious step given in this chapter. The facts are:-

When the battle is hot enemies will flee mostly if the casualty on their side is heavy. When blood flows in the battle field enemies will surrender and flee. This is what happens, when the Psalmist says, **"The righteous will be glad when they are avenged, when they bathe their feet in the blood of the wicked" Psalm 58:10** To bathe your feet in the blood of the enemy means the wicked are dead and shall rise no more.

Brethren, fear no color do not entertain fear in the heart. Even if the battle is fierce, the Lord shall see you through. The Bible says, **"When evil men advance against me to devour my flesh, when**

my enemies and my foes attack me, they will stumble and fall. Though an army besieges me, my heart will not fear; though war break out against me, even then will I be confident. Psalm 27:2-3 Build confidence and face the enemy, use the armory in your hands against them, and they shall flee. They will call 911, but there won't be response.

Mind you, the wicked are confident, proud and naughty. They won't stay long before they fade away. The bible says, **"For a little while they are exalted, and then they are gone; they are brought low and gathered up like all others; they are brought low and gathered up like all others; they are cut off like heads of grain. Job 24:24.** Enemies that rise up against you shall surely meet their waterloo. Yours is to fight the battle with zeal in prayer. They shall be defeated and be annihilated. Believe me, the enemy shall die and rise no more. **"He will never come to his house again; his place will know him no more".** **Psalm 7:10**. His co-criminals in the act will be left in the dark forever in the name of Jesus.

Untimely death is the food and bread of the wicked. They are enemies that don't stay long. **"A little while and the wicked will be no more;**

though you look for them, they will not be found" Psalm 37:10

In summary, the wicked hunts people in the spirit and in real life. The Philistine brought Samson down through the lap of Delilah. Philistines have been a long- time adversary of Israel. Though Samson was powerful, a woman sold him out to the hands of the enemy. Haman became thorn in the flesh of Mordecia, without cause, Haman the wicked hanged himself in the gallow he prepared for Mordecia. Shimei cursed David when he fled Jerusalem to the unknown as a result of the revolt of his son, Absalom; Shimei did this because he was a Benjamin, Saul's tribe, who lost out to David. Shimei was aggressive; he tagged David a usurper and rained curses on him. Eventually, when David returned, the enemy Shimei paid with his life. Judas Iscariot made a sudden U turn and sold Jesus into the hands of the enemy who crucified him, but then Judas Iscariot paid supreme price for this. He hanged himself. When the children of Israel were in Egypt, they were turned to slaves, and later were turned to enemy. When Moses rise to the situation as God sent him to free them, Pharaoh refused. The Egyptians paid supreme price for this. Egyptian soldiers and their chariots perished in the Red Sea. At Mount Carmel contest, Elijah made the enemies of God who worshipped Baal, rather than Yahweh pay supreme price when their idol could not save them. Any herbalist, witchdoctor, wizard, witch or sorcerer that rise up against you shall pay the supreme price of paralysis, shame, madness, blindness, deafness and death, if they refuse to let you go. When it happens you shall boast and say, "Dial 911 and see if your god will answer you" As it happened in Mount Carmel in the days of Elijah, so shall they fail woefully and die, in the name of Jesus.

Surely, enemies will rise the wicked will not fold arms. What can make enemies shiver, before they can surrender or be silent? The followings are important:

1. When enemies rise and you are prayerful, enemies will flee and surrender.
2. When enemies rise and you take your case to God, enemies will be silenced.
3. When enemies arise and you cry to God in the order of children of Israel in captivity in Egypt, enemies will be drowned.
4. When enemies rise and you cry to God in the order of David, when the Amalekites strike and

took his men, children and women away, enemies will be overpowered and be defeated.

5. When enemies arise and you rebuke them, they shall flee in the order before Archangel Michael that rebuked Satan in Jude 1:9. **"But even the archangel Michael, when he was disputing with the devil about the body of Moses, did not dare to bring a slanderous accusation against him, but said, "The Lord rebuke you!".**

6. When enemies arise and you fast, they shall be put to shame. Satan came tempting Jesus after 40 days and 40 nights of fasting and prayer. Jesus silenced him.

7. When enemies arise and you praise God, you will overcome in the like of Paul and Silas. They praised God and the Angels visited them in prison and they were set free to the shame of devil. No wonder it is said, be not hot in prayer and cold in praises. Praise is the best of all sacrifice and the true evidence of godliness.

8. When enemies arise to kill you and you believe in the Lord, what you pronounce shall come to pass. Jezebel dared to kill Elijah, after Mount Carmel contest. Elijah pronounced there won't be rain or dew for 3years and it came to pass.

9. When enemies arise and see light of God in you, they shall rise no more.

10. When enemies arise and see blood of Jesus on you, they shall tremble and turn back. The children of Israel put blood of the Lamb on the door post and death passed over them.

11. When enemies arise and meet you on your knee praying, they shall surrender and turn back. You are tall than enemy on your knee. When a good man falls, he falls on his knees.

12. When enemies arise to inflict you with famine and you lift your eyes to God in prayer for open heaven, enemy shall fail because prayer is the key to heavenly treasures.

Prayer is the great engine to overthrow enemy. It is time to pray and seek the face of God. Men and women of God are always men and women of prayer. You don't fold your arms when enemies arise; the fact is you should be at alert all the time. Don't allow enemy to strike before you take action. Jesus selected His twelve disciples after all-night prayer. He knew Satan will strike thereafter. He prepared the foundation of his ministry with prayer. He never wait until Satan strike. Judas Iscariot lost out because he was not in the prayer ground with Jesus. He wondered away. Your attitude to life, your habit, your position with God, your closeness to the Word; determines how you will tackle situation at hand.

In all, prayer is what you need most, in as much you understand the Word and keep away from sin. Prayer is a strong wall and fortress to rely on against the adversary of the wicked. No wonder, prayer is called the key of the day and lock of the night.

When enemies arise; pray. It is your life line to a fulfilled destiny. Your destiny is at stake, if you can't pray. No matter the storms of life, they all bow to the power of prayer. Prayer makes you bold and fierce against adversaries. Prayer equips you against mountains and barriers. Prayer is like a threshing machine against a mountain or rock. You break it to pieces and dust in prayer. Every mountain bows before prayer. That mountain is the enemy that rises against you.

Nothing just happen! Prayer makes it happen! Enemies won't turn back if you don't pray. Enemies won't surrender if you are prayer less. Enemies won't bow to superior power in the absence of prayer. Enemies won't surrender if you slumber. Enemies shall arise if you fold arms and refuse to stretch your hands to God in prayer.

If you don't want to settle for less you must learn the act of prayer. If you want God's plan for you, go into prayer. No matter the devices of the devil, concentrate in prayer. If you want to tear the devil up everywhere you walk; go into prayer.

What shall we do if enemies arise? What step shall we take? Where shall we run to? The truth is, every believer must be found in the business of prayer. Enemy will not rise if he doesn't see good seed to kill in you; if he doesn't see flourishing plantation in the garden of your life. A star must be there to kill before enemies arise and attack. A destiny must be buoyant before he strikes. So, when enemy strikes or rise up against you, know that something tangible is planted in you.

PRAYER POINTS

1. I thank my God who will not allow affliction to rise up again in my life, in the name of Jesus.
2. I thank you Lord, for your protection and mercy upon me in the name of Jesus.

3. O Lord, forgive me every sin that makes enemy have upper hand in my life, in the name of Jesus.

4. Lord Jesus, have mercy upon me and forgive me sins that open door for enemy in my life, in the name of Jesus.

5. Blood of Jesus, heal me of wounds I sustain when enemy rise against me, in the name of Jesus.

6. I drink blood of Jesus, to neutralize and destroy evil deposit in my life, in the name of Jesus.

7. O Lord, wash my heart clean of sin in the name of Jesus.

8. Holy Ghost power, draw me close to you, in the name of Jesus.

9. Holy Spirit, equip me with warfare equipment to destroy works of darkness, in the name of Jesus.

10. Powers assigned to kill my vision, my life is not your candidate; expire, in the name of Jesus.

11. O Lord, give me power to dominate and destroy works of darkness, in the name of Jesus.

12. Power to live a righteous life come upon me, so that I may live above dark powers dedicated against me, in the name of Jesus.

13. Every wickedness in my heart, come out and die, in the name of Jesus.

14. Any wicked power assigned to change the course of my destiny, die and rise no more, in the name of Jesus.

15. Powers making life difficult for me so that I may reap failure at the edge of breakthrough expire and rise no more in the name of Jesus.

16. Every wicked power keeping watch at the door post of my door, paralyze and die, in the name of Jesus.

17. Powers and forces of darkness that commit evil at will your time is up, die and rise no more, in the name of Jesus.

18. Every sin in my life that open door of attack to my life, expire, in the name of Jesus.

19. Every injustice done to my life, be nullified in the name of Jesus.

20. Every wickedness of the wicked assigned to reduce my virtue to nothing, die, in the name of Jesus.

21. O Lord, break every curse pronounced upon by my adversaries, in the name of Jesus.

22. O Lord, if you curse my lineage in the past forgive us O Lord, in the name of Jesus.

23. Every toughness against me scatter and backfire, O Lord let their evil plan swallow them, in the name of Jesus.

24. O Lord, separate wickedness from my heart, in the name of Jesus.
25. Spirit to avoid trouble and live a holy life, envelope my life, in the name of Jesus.
26. Every battle against my soul, scatter and backfire against powers behind it, let them fall and rise no more, in the name of Jesus.
27. I fire arrow of God against powers assigned to kill me and command them to fall down and rise no more, in the name of Jesus.
28. O Lord, let heavy casualty happen on the side of enemies after my life, in the name of Jesus.
29. Angels of God, arise, strike down enemies fighting me in my sleep, let their blood flow like water, in the name of Jesus.
30. Enemies of my soul, I fire you, turn back, flee and die, and rise no more, in the name of Jesus.
31. O Lord, give me large heart to fight my enemy and overcome them in the name of Jesus.
32. Enemies of my soul that refuse to leave me alone, I kill you and bath my feet with your blood, in the name of Jesus.
33. Woe to enemies and foes that rise to attack me, in the name of Jesus.
34. Every stubborn pursuer after my life summersault and die, in the name of Jesus.

35. Dark army assigned to attack, I fire you, die and rise no more, in the name of Jesus.
36. Every warfare against me, scatter, in the name of Jesus.
37. O Lord, turn the pride of the wicked to shame, in the name of Jesus.
38. Enemies of my soul, fade away, in the name of Jesus.
39. O Lord, let the obituary of powers against my soul be announced in the name of Jesus.
40. Angels of God; cut the head of powers that determine to kill me, in the spirit, in the name of Jesus.
41. Every barrier erected to stop my breakthrough, scatter, in the name of Jesus.
42. Every Philistine against my Samson, die and rise no more in the name of Jesus.
43. Every Haman against my Moddecia, die and rise no more, in the name of Jesus.
44. Every Shimei assigned to curse my David, be cut off with your curse, in the name of Jesus.
45. Every Judas Iscariot on the way to sell me to the wicked be hanged, in the name of Jesus.
46. Every Pharaoh that vow, he will not let me go, die in the Red Sea, in the name of Jesus.

47. My Elijah, kill every power that worship and consult other gods, to attack me, in the name of Jesus.
48. Witch doctor, in charge of my case; fall down and die in the name of Jesus.
49. Witchcraft powers that gathered for my sake in order to terminate my life, scatter in the name of Jesus.
50. I fire arrows of paralysis against the wicked assign to terminate me, in the name of Jesus.
51. Arrow of prayerlessness fired against me backfire in the name of Jesus.
52. O Lord, I cry unto you, enemies surround me, fight for me, in the name of Jesus.
53. My destiny in captivity of the enemy; wake up, receive heavenly power and walk out of captivity, in the name of Jesus.
54. I pursue, I overtake and destroy my enemies and possess my possession, in the name of Jesus.
55. Powers assigned to rebuke me, even after death, my Angel Michael rebuke you, paralyze and die, in the name of Jesus.
56. O Lord, put your praises in my mouth and let my enemies scatter and be defeated, in the name of Jesus.

57. Spirit to fast and pray in the order of Jesus, and overcome Satan, come upon me, in the name of Jesus.

58. My spirit in the prison of darkness, be released, and strike my enemies to death, in the name of Jesus.

59. O Lord, anoint my tongue against my enemies, let them fall and rise no more, in the name of Jesus.

60. As from today, there won't be rain or dew, in the camp of the enemy in the name of Jesus.

61. Light of God, overshadow me now, and let enemies around me scatter, in the name of Jesus.

62. Blood of Jesus, be a mark on my forehead that chase enemies away, in the name of Jesus.

63. Sudden death shall pass over me, in the name of Jesus.

64. Every failure assign for me in the spirit, expire, in the name of Jesus.

65. O Lord, put engine of prayer in my heart and body, in the name of Jesus.

66. O Lord, turn my house to house of prayer, in the name of Jesus.

67. Enemy of my soul I strike you before you strike me in the name of Jesus.

68. O Lord, marry me with the Word, my Bible and Hoy Spirit, in the name of Jesus.

69. Wall of prayer, fortress of prayer surround me and protect me in the name of Jesus.

70. Every storm introduced to my life, expire, in the name of Jesus.

71. Every mountain and barrier assigned to humiliate me to stagnation, expire in the name of Jesus.

72. Powers assigned to rubbish my destiny, die and rise no more, in the name of Jesus.

73. Adversaries tormenting my life; expire, appear no more in the name of Jesus.

74. My prayer, turn to threshing machine, break every mountain, barrier and dark rock that surround me, in the name of Jesus.

75. Enemies around me, surrender in the name of Jesus.

CHAPTER 2

DEALING WITH HOUSEHOLD ENEMY AND ENVIRONMENTAL ATTACK

Micah 7:8

8. Do not gloat over me, my enemy! Though I have fallen, I will rise. Though I sit in darkness, the LORD will be my light.

Jeremiah 17:18

18. Let my persecutors be put to shame, but keep me from shame; let them be terrified, but keep me from terror. Bring on them the day of disaster; destroy them with double destruction.

Numbers 23:23

23. There is no divination against Jacob, no evil omens against Israel. It will now be said of Jacob and of Israel, 'See what God has done!'

Isaiah 54:17

17. No weapon forged against you will prevail, and you will refute every tongue that accuses you. This is the heritage of the servants of the LORD, and this is their vindication from me," declares the LORD.

PRAYER POINTS

1. I thank my God, for he silenced household enemies after my life, in the name of Jesus.
2. I praise my God, who subdued environmental forces that are against my advancement, in the name of Jesus.
3. O Lord, I thank you for breaking barriers of the enemy against my success, in the name of Jesus.
4. Lord Jesus, forgive sins that attract household enemies to pursue me, in the name of Jesus.
5. Environmental power taking my sins to attack me, your time is up, my God has forgiven me, in the name of Jesus.
6. I cover myself with blood of Jesus against attack of environmental forces, in the name of Jesus.
7. I drink blood of Jesus to purge me of evil deposit in my system in the name of Jesus.
8. Blood of Jesus, flow in my life as barricade against arrows of darkness in the name of Jesus.
9. Holy Spirit Divine, empower me against attacks of household powers, in the name of Jesus.
10. Holy Ghost Fire, consume powers that vow I shall not make it in life, in the name of Jesus.

11. O Lord, strike household enemies that consult other gods to harm me, let them paralyze and rise no more, in the name of Jesus.

12. When my God visits the bloodthirsty after me with terror, they collapse and rise no more in the name of Jesus.

13. Holy Ghost, sweep away enemies with burning coals of the broom tree, let them expire and rise no more, in the name of Jesus.

14. Every arrow fired against my household backfire to the sender, let them fall and rise no more, in the name of Jesus.

15. Deceit tongues that rise up against me, I pull you off, let the power fall and rise no more, in the name of Jesus.

16. Principalities and powers that rise against my household shall fail and expire, they shall rise no more, in the name of Jesus.

17. I struck down powers waiting for me to serve punishment in the spirit, they shall fall and rise no more, in the name of Jesus.

18. O Lord, inflict vengeance on powers that is against my household, let them fall and rise no more in the name of Jesus.

19. I cut to pieces every enemy of my life with double-edge sword in my hand; they fall and rise no more, in the name of Jesus.

20. Those who stand on my way to make music to my God; shall fail and rise no more in the name of Jesus.

21. Those that say my household will not praise my God with dance shall not know peace, but shall fall and rise no more in the name of Jesus.

22. Those that say my household will not be glad in the King of kings, shall not prosper, but fall and rise no more in the name of Jesus.

23. Powers that vow my household shall not sing new song shall fail woefully and rise no more, in the name of Jesus.

24. My God shall break chains and fetters in my life while my enemies shall faint, fall and rise no more, in the name of Jesus.

25. My God shall deliver me from household wickedness, as a surprise they shall faint and rise no more, in the name of Jesus.

26. I rejoice in the Lord for his protection over me, my household enemy saw it and collapse, they shall rise no more, in the name of Jesus.

27. I refuse to put hope in men/women but put hope in my God, enemies are mad at me, they shall fall and rise no more, in the name of Jesus.

28. Today is the day, the plans of enemy shall come to nothing, they shall depart to the ground and rise no more, in the name of Jesus.

29. Unfaithful people around me are unhappy, I serve a faithful God, they conspired but scatter and rise no more, in the name of Jesus.

30. I worship God who upholds the cause of the oppressed, enemies rise against me, they fell and rise no more, in the name of Jesus.

31. The Lord who uphold the cause of the oppressed is my God, enemies are furious at me, they fell and rise no more, in the name of Jesus.

32. My God is a God who gives food to the poor, enemies attack me of this, but they fell and rise no more, in the name of Jesus.

33. I serve God who sets prisoner free, but powers that captivate life arise to imprison me and my family, they fell and rise no more in the name of Jesus.

34. I serve God who gives decree that never pass away, it favours my household, enemies are angry, but my God silenced them forever.

35. O Lord, attack my enemies with lightening and hailstone, let them pass away, so that I see them no more, in the name of Jesus.

36. O Lord, let heavenly snow and cloud swallow enemies that rise up against me, let them fall and rise no more in the name of Jesus.

37. O Lord, consume enemies that rise against me with stormy winds, let them fall and rise no more, in the name of Jesus.

38. My God is good, I shall eat the fruit of my labour, if enemies rise, they shall fall and rise no more, in the name of Jesus.

39. Wild animals that rise against me shall fail and rise no more in the name of Jesus.

40. Wild birds that fly against my household shall fall and die, and rise no more, in the name of Jesus.

41. Strange creatures assign to eat the fruit of my labour, shall die and rise no more in the name of Jesus.

42. Powers that vow I will not command God's work from one generation to another, your time is up, fall down and rise no more in the name of Jesus.

43. As the mountains surround Jerusalem, so the Lord surround my family from calamity in the name of Jesus.

44. O Lord, come and save my household from environmental attack, let the attackers, fall and rise no more, in the name of Jesus.

45. My enemies; eat the bread of tears you prepare for me, fall and rise no more in the name of Jesus.

46. Enemies waiting to mock my household were disappointed, they fall and rise no more in the name of Jesus

47. O Lord, shine your face upon us and let my enemies sober, paralyze and fall, in the name of Jesus.

48. O Lord, drive out spiritual forces with whip, let them scatter, fall and rise no more, in the name of Jesus.

49. Environmental powers assigned to burn down my properties; I rebuke you, perish and rise no more, in the name of Jesus.

50. Every foreign god in my household, die and rise no more, in the name of Jesus.

51. Territorial alliance against me; scatter and rise no more in the name of Jesus.

52. Environmental forces after my household, perish in disgrace in the name of Jesus.

53. Those that consult other gods to attack me shall fail woefully and rise no more in the name of Jesus.

54. O Lord, scatter the band of ruthless men and women that seeks my life, let them expire, in the name of Jesus.

55. O Lord, let my household be yours forever, never shall other powers take over my house,

they shall fade away forever in the name of Jesus.

56. O Lord, avenge those that vow to scatter my house, let them scatter and rise no more, in the name of Jesus.

57. O Lord, silence the proud that rise up against me, in the name of Jesus.

58. The wicked that jubilate against my house, shall fail and fall, and rise no more, in the name of Jesus.

59. The wicked that rise to crush my house shall fail and rise no more in the name of Jesus.

60. Murderers in the spirit, targeting my household, fall by the sword and rise no more, in the name of Jesus.

61. O Lord, cast the throne of enemy to the ground and render them useless, in the name of Jesus.

62. O Lord, turn oppressors that are against my household to senseless one among people, let them rise no more in the name of Jesus.

63. O Lord, let the fools against my house be fools, until they fall and rise no more, in the name of Jesus.

64. O Lord, grant my family relief till a pit is dug for my enemy, in the name of Jesus.

65. O Lord, do not forsake me in the battle of life, in the name of Jesus.

66. O Lord, rise up and support my household against the wicked in the name of Jesus.
67. Every misery organized for me, expire and rise no more in the name of Jesus.
68. Those that band together against my home shall fail woefully and rise no more in the name of Jesus.
69. Powers planning for the heart of my family go astray to other gods, die and rise no more, in the name of Jesus.
70. My household is well established in the Lord; it shall not be moved, in the name of Jesus.
71. O Lord let cloud and darkness of evil around my household clear away, let my enemies be defeated, in the name of Jesus.
72. O Lord, let every mountain around my household melt like wax before fire, let my enemies expire, in the name of Jesus.
73. My household will rejoice and be glad in the Lord and so shall it be in the name of Jesus. Amen.

CHAPTER 3

DEALING WITH ENEMIES THAT RISE UP AGAINST DESTINY

Joel 2:26-27

26. You will have plenty to eat, until you are full, and you will praise the name of the LORD your God, who has worked wonders for you; never again will my people be shamed.

27. Then you will know that I am in Israel, that I am the LORD your God, and that there is no other; never again will my people be shamed.

Exodus 14:13-14

13. Moses answered the people, "Do not be afraid. Stand firm and you will see the deliverance the LORD will bring you today. The Egyptians you see today you will never see again.

14. The LORD will fight for you; you need only to be still."

Psalm 4:7

7. You have filled my heart with greater joy than when their grain and new wine abound.

PRAYER POINTS

1. O Lord, I thank you for protecting me against enemies that vow I will not make it in life, in the name of Jesus.

2. I thank you Lord, for your mercy and love for me, in the name of Jesus.

3. O Lord, I come before you for mercy and forgiveness, let it come to pass in my life, in the name of Jesus.

4. O Lord, don't look at my previous sin, or else, I will be a failure, have mercy upon me in the name of Jesus.

5. I cover myself with blood of Jesus, enemies that rise up against me shall faint and fall, in the name of Jesus.

6. Blood of Jesus, be a demarcation between me and the enemy of my soul in the name of Jesus.

7. Holy Ghost Fire, burn to ashes every enemy that rise up against my destiny, in the name of Jesus.

8. Holy Spirit, lead my step right, in the name of Jesus.

9. Powers that rise up against me because I do not walk in the counsel of the wicked, shall fall and rise no more in the name of Jesus.

10. The Lord is on my side, any man or woman that attack me shall fall and rise no more, in the name of Jesus.

11. The Lord is on my side, when the anger of enemy flared against me they fail and fall, never to rise again in the name of Jesus.

12. Powers assigned to swallow me fail and fall, never shall you rise again, in the name of Jesus.

13. Dark flood assign to engulf me, dry up, never shall you rise again in the name of Jesus.

14. Witchcraft watchman monitoring me shall fall and rise no more in the name of Jesus.

15. Those that vow that in vain shall I wake early and stay up late to get good things of life shall fail and rise no more, in the name of Jesus.

16. Any power that vow I shall not be a chosen instrument of God, shall fail and rise no more, in the name of Jesus.

17. Any power assign to use me as instrument of darkness, I am not your candidate, fall down and rise no more, in Jesus name.

18. My glory, it is time you rise and shine, let enemies of my destiny fall apart and rise no more, in the name of Jesus.

19. O Lord, rescue me from the hand of the wicked and let them rise no more, in the name of Jesus.

20. O Lord, make my friend understand nothing and know nothing until they fall, in the name of Jesus.
21. O Lord, pull out the wicked that walk about in darkness against me, and be disgraced, in the name of Jesus.
22. Those who come together as one to destroy me, shall be destroyed, in the name of Jesus.
23. O Lord, let those who rise in alliance against me, perish and be like refuse on the ground, in the name of Jesus.
24. Those that plan to destroy my destiny, perish and be like chaff before the wind, in the name of Jesus.
25. O Lord, strike all my enemies on the jaw, let them collapse and rise no more, in the name of Jesus.
26. The wicked standing in judgment against me shall fail, they shall rise no more, in the name of Jesus.
27. Every conspiracy and plot of the enemy against me shall fail and scatter and they shall rise no more, in the name of Jesus.
28. God of Elijah, arise with fire, consume those that vow I will not fulfill my destiny, in the name of Jesus.

29. As fire consume the forest, so shall enemies of my destiny be consumed and rise no more, in the name of Jesus.

30. As flames set the mountains ablaze so shall enemies of my soul, be consumed in the name of Jesus.

31. Angels of God, pursue my pursuer until they fall and rise no more, in the name of Jesus.

32. O God arise; terrify enemy of my soul with storm, and let them rise no more, in the name of Jesus.

33. O God arise, pursue the enemy of my destiny with your tempest, let them rise no more, in the name of Jesus.

34. O God, cover; the face of my enemies with shame, let them faint, fall and rise no more, in the name of Jesus.

35. O Lord, put away your displeasure towards me and enlarge my coast, let my enemies turn away from pursuing me in the name of Jesus.

36. My God turns to me and have mercy on me, my enemies were terrified, they fell and rise no more.

37. O Lord, support me in every battle against my enemy, let them fall and rise no more, in the name of Jesus.

38. O Lord, cut off the splendor of the enemy over me, strangulate them, let them rise no more, in the name of Jesus.

39. O Lord, cover my enemy with mantle of shame, let their time expire by fire, in the name of Jesus.

40. O Lord, let your wrath burn like fire against my enemies, in the name of Jesus.

41. Those that taunt, and mock me shall fail woefully, in the name of Jesus.

42. O Lord, set my destiny on firm foundation that enemy cannot attack or pull down, let them fall and rise no more in the name of Jesus.

43. Every voice speaking against my destiny, backfire in the name of Jesus.

44. Where is the Lord God of Elijah? Arise; speak against powers assign to ruin me, let them fall and rise no more in the name of Jesus.

45. Wicked prophecy assigned to shorten my life backfire, in the name of Jesus.

46. Thou snare of too late holding me back, break in the name of Jesus.

47. Destiny killers advancing at me, in order to scatter my destiny, die and rise no more in the name of Jesus.

48. Holy Ghost Fire, burn to ashes every file and document used to monitor my life, in the name of Jesus.

49. Rain of affliction targeted at my destiny, stop by fire, in the name of Jesus.

50. Stubborn witchcraft dedicated against my destiny die and rise no more in the name of Jesus.

51. Every ritual carried out to turn my destiny upside down, catch fire and roast to ashes, in the name of Jesus.

52. I will tread upon the lion and the cobra, they shall not harm me, my enemy shall die in gap for it, in the name of Jesus.

53. O Lord, rescue me from the mouth of wild lion, strike it down, let it rise no more in the name of Jesus.

54. Dark seas that lifted pounding waves against my destiny, scatter and rise no more, in the name of Jesus.

55. Generation evil contract signed by my ancestors, holding me captive, be nullified by the power in the blood of Jesus.

56. Witchcraft padlock fashioned against my destiny, break in the name of Jesus.

57. Marine witchcraft opposition against my destiny, scatter in the name of Jesus.

58. Witchcraft pot holding my destiny captive, break in the name of Jesus.

59. Witchcraft influence against my destiny, scatter in the name of Jesus.

60. Every satanic wickedness in the heavenlies against my destiny, scatter and rise no more, in the name of Jesus.

61. Devourers of destiny; my destiny is not your candidate, therefore, leave me alone and die, in the name of Jesus.

62. Every satanic agenda for my destiny, scatter and rise no more in the name of Jesus.

63. Thou power of frustration and backwardness planted in my foundation, expire and rise no more, in the name of Jesus.

64. All those waiting to see my shame shall be put to shame, in the name of Jesus.

65. My destiny shall not fellowship with failure, in the name of Jesus.

66. Anointing of excellence locate my destiny in the name of Jesus.

67. I withdraw my destiny from evil altar, and command evil priest in charge to fall down and rise no more, in the name of Jesus.

68. Heavenly angels provoke my enlargement and success in the name of Jesus.

69. Witchcraft opposition against my destiny, scatter and rise no more, in the name of Jesus.

70. My destiny; find rest in the Lord, and my enemies shall scatter and surrender, in the name of Jesus.

71. I shall be like a tree planted by streams of water that yields its fruit in season, in the name of Jesus.

CHAPTER 4

DEALING WITH ENEMIES THAT RISE UP AGAINST YOUR HEALTH

Jeremiah 30:16-17

16. "'But all who devour you will be devoured; all your enemies will go into exile. Those who plunder you will be plundered; all who make spoil of you I will despoil.

17. But I will restore you to health and heal your wounds,' declares the LORD, 'because you are called an outcast, Zion for whom no one cares.'

Isaiah 28:18

18. Your covenant with death will be annulled; your agreement with the realm of the dead will not stand. When the overwhelming scourge sweeps by, you will be beaten down by it.

Psalm 91:15-16

15. He will call on me, and I will answer him; I will be with him in trouble, I will deliver him and honor him.

16. With long life I will satisfy him and show him my salvation. "

PRAYER POINTS

1. O Lord, I thank you for keeping me healthy today in the name of Jesus.
2. Lord Jesus, receive my thanksgiving for your stripes that make me whole.
3. Lord Jesus, lay hands of forgiveness upon me so that good health may be my portion, in the name of Jesus.
4. O Lord forgive me, let your healing power be upon me, in the name of Jesus.
5. I drink blood of Jesus to sanitize me and purge me of evil deposit in the name of Jesus.
6. I cover myself with blood of Jesus against every arrow of darkness in the name of Jesus.
7. O Lord, let Holy Spirit fill me afresh, in the name of Jesus.
8. Holy Spirit, come down upon me, in the name of Jesus
9. My God heals me, when my bones were in agony, enemies saw it, they were shocked, they fall and rise no more in Jesus name.

10. My God healed my soul in anguish, my enemies saw it, they fainted, fall and rise no more, in Jesus name.

11. I worship God who heals the brokenhearted, enemies are furious at me, they rise but scatter and rise no more.

12. My God binds my wounds, he healed my wound, but enemies are unhappy, they fell and rise no more.

13. Powers that vow I will go down to the pit, you are not my God, perish with your boast, and rise no more, in the name of Jesus.

14. Powers assign to make me a man without strength shall fail woefully, in the name of Jesus.

15. Powers assign to set me apart with the dead, I am not your candidate, fall down and paralyze and rise no more, in the name of Jesus.

16. Powers that vow I will be treated like slain who lie in the grave, shall meet double failure and rise no more, in the name of Jesus.

17. Powers that say I shall be remembered no more shall fail woefully in the name of Jesus.

18. I shall not be a candidate cut off from the care of the Lord, in the name of Jesus.

19. Powers assigned to keep me in the darkest depth of the world shall fall and rise no more, in the name of Jesus.
20. Every wave of darkness assign to swallow me expire; and rise no more in the name of Jesus.
21. Powers that vow I will lose my immediate friends to cold arm of death shall fail and rise no more, in the name of Jesus.
22. O Lord, save me from the power of the grave, let my enemy replace me, and be buried in the name of Jesus.
23. O Lord, do not sweep me away in my sleep to death but silence enemies that so wish me, in the name of Jesus.
24. O Lord, don't consume me in your anger, but keep me alive, let powers that vow to consume me fall and rise no more, in the name of Jesus.
25. I shall not moan nor mourn to strange death, in the name of Jesus.
26. O Lord, deliver me from deadly sword of the enemy, let them fall by their sword and rise no more, in the name of Jesus.
27. O Lord, break the teeth of the wicked assign to bite my flesh in the spirit, let them collapse and rise no more, in the name of Jesus.

28. O Lord, give me relief from stress caused by enemies, strike them let them rise no more, in the name of Jesus.

29. My God delivered me from the depths of the grave, I live, my enemy fainted, and rise no more, in the name of Jesus.

30. Dark powers that rise against my health shall rise no more, they shall fall and never rise in the name of Jesus.

31. Powers that vow my days on earth shall be of trouble and sorrow; shall not prosper but fail in the name of Jesus.

32. Every deadly pestilence waiting to consume me, expire let powers behind it fall and rise no more, in the name of Jesus.

33. Every terror of the night organized to torment me, expire and rise no more in the name of Jesus.

34. My God promised no harm will befall me, those who plot harm for me shall fall by it, in the name of Jesus.

35. It is written, no disaster will come near my tent, those who plan disaster shall fall by it, in the name of Jesus.

36. Those who worship idol to torment my health, I am not your candidate, fall and rise no more in the name of Jesus.

37. Sickness that will make me forget or reject food; shall not be my portion in the name of Jesus.

38. O Lord, save me from sickness that will reduce me to skin and bones, in the name of Jesus.

39. Witchcraft owl on the mission to announce my death, die and catch fire and roast to ashes, in the name of Jesus.

40. A thousand may fall at my side as a result of evil arrow, it shall not come near me, I will not fall in the name of Jesus.

41. Every sickbed enemy prepared for me in the spirit, catch fire and roast to ashes, in the name of Jesus.

42. Pit of sickness dug for me by agent of darkness; consume your digger in the name of Jesus.

43. Every power oppressing my life by agents of sickness and disease, expire in the name of Jesus.

44. Every unconscious gift that leads to sickness, catch fire and roast to ashes, let the owners expire in my life, in the name of Jesus.

45. Every arrow of terminal sickness in my life, come out, I fire you back to the sender, in the name of Jesus.

46. Every power that vow I will die of terminal sickness, you are not my God, die with your vow in the name of Jesus.
47. Every decree of bad health assigned to consume, break in the name of Jesus.
48. Every power that links my health to evil sacrifice, die in the name of Jesus.
49. By the grace of God, I shall not die, but live to witness the sweetness of the Lord Almighty God.
50. I speak life unto every organ of my body and command my enemies to scatter, in the name of Jesus.
51. Spirit of sickness, quit my life, in the name of Jesus.
52. Every arrow that flies about against my health, backfire and consume your sender, in the name of Jesus.
53. Every arrow of calamity fired against me backfire to your sender and destroy them, in the name of Jesus.
54. Every arrow of untimely death fired against me, backfire to your sender and replace me in the grave, in the name of Jesus.
55. Plagues that destroy, I am not your candidate; expire in the name of Jesus.

56. Every snare of sickness, set up to destroy my life, catch fire and roast to ashes, in the name of Jesus.

57. Every satanic device assigned to multiply sickness in my body, break and catch fire in the name of Jesus.

58. Every tree of sickness growing in the garden of my life be uprooted in the name of Jesus.

59. Every power announcing my name in sickbay, fall down and die, and rise no more, in the name of Jesus.

60. Every coven of sickness catch fire in the name of Jesus.

61. Every spiritual father, treating me with evil medication, drink your medicine and die, in the name of Jesus.

62. Every spiritual mother, treating me with evil medication, drink your medicine and die in the name of Jesus.

63. Every spiritual In-law, treating me with evil medication, drink your medicine and die, in the name of Jesus.

64. Every stranger in the spirit, treating me with evil medication drink your medicine and die, in the name of Jesus.

65. Powers assigned to cripple my health, paralyze and die, in the name of Jesus.

66. Excesses of darkness in my health life, dry up in the name of Jesus.
67. I break the law of bad health in my life, in the name of Jesus.
68. O Lord, open rivers of healing upon my life in the name of Jesus.
69. O Lord, open rivers of good health upon my life in the name of Jesus.
70. I praise my God, who redeems my life from pit of darkness, I live and my enemies shall be devoured, in the name of Jesus.
71. I praise my God, who forgives all sins and heal all diseases, in the name of Jesus.

CHAPTER 5

DEALING WITH ENEMIES THAT RISE UP AGAINST CAREER AND CALLING

Joel 2:28-30

28. "And afterward, I will pour out my Spirit on all people. Your sons and daughters will prophesy, your old men will dream dreams, your young men will see visions.

29. Even on my servants, both men and women, I will pour out my Spirit in those days.

30. I will show wonders in the heavens and on the earth, blood and fire and billows of smoke.

Isaiah 40:29-31

29. He gives strength to the weary and increases the power of the weak.

30. Even youths grow tired and weary, and young men stumble and fall;

31. But those who hope in the LORD will renew their strength. They will soar on wings like eagles; they will run and not grow weary, they will walk and not be faint.

Isaiah 54:14-15

14. In righteousness you will be established: Tyranny will be far from you; you will have nothing to fear. Terror will be far removed; it will not come near you.

15. If anyone does attack you, it will not be my doing; whoever attacks you will surrender to you.

PRAYER POINTS

1. I thank you Lord for lifting me when I fall in the name of Jesus
2. I praise my God, who will never leave me or forsake me in the name of Jesus.
3. Lord Jesus, forgive me every sin that makes me stagnant in my career and calling in the name of Jesus.
4. Lord Jesus, forgive me for not being prayerful enough in the name of Jesus.
5. Blood of Jesus, cover my career and calling from attack in the name of Jesus.
6. I cover myself with blood of Jesus, to make more than a conqueror in the name of Jesus.

7. Holy Spirit, make my calling, your calling in the name of Jesus.

8. Holy Spirit, support my heavenly career and favour me in the name of Jesus.

9. Any power that is against my going to the house of God to pray shall fail and fall, and rise no more in the name of Jesus.

10. Any power assign to debar me from entering house of worship, shall paralyze and rise no more in the name of Jesus.

11. O Lord; have mercy upon me, let those who oppose me, fall and never rise again in the name of Jesus.

12. O Lord, since you forgave my iniquities, enemies are not happy, O Lord send them on journey of no return in the name of Jesus.

13. O Lord, let your wrath be upon my enemies that oppose my calling, let them flee forever, in the name of Jesus.

14. O Lord, let your fierce anger be upon powers that oppose my career, let them be destroyed and rise no more, in the name of Jesus.

15. As I receive salvation of the Lord, my enemies shall rise no more against me, in the name of Jesus.

16. O Lord, pour anointing of revival upon my head, and let my enemy fall and rise no more in the name of Jesus.

17. Any power that does not want me to listen to what God the Lord says, fall down and rise no more, in the name of Jesus.

18. Any power annoyed of the unfailing love of God for me, fall down and rise no more, in the name of Jesus.

19. Those annoyed of the glory of God upon me, perish and rise no more in the name of Jesus.

20. Powers planning I will fail in faith and return to folly, shall not stand but perish and rise no more, in the name of Jesus.

21. Those who against love and faithfulness to meet together in my life, shall fail and fall, never to rise again, in the name of Jesus.

22. Those who are not happy for righteousness and peace to kiss each other in my life, shall fall and rise no more, in the name of Jesus.

23. O Lord, maintain my right among my enemies and let them rise no more against me, in the name of Jesus.

24. O Lord, give me an undivided heart that will make your child and make enemy faint and rise no more, in the name of Jesus.

25. O Lord, grant me your strength, let me rise above my enemy, let them fall and rise no more, in the name of Jesus.

26. O Lord, lead me to your holy mountain where you set your foundation, and let enemy of my soul fall and rise no more.

27. O Lord, anoint me with your sacred oil of greatness, in the name of Jesus.

28. O Lord, anoint me with sacred oil of healing that will make my enemy shut up and rise no more, in the name of Jesus.

29. O Lord, anoint me with sacred oil of prosperity that will baffle enemies and make them surrender for life in the name of Jesus.

30. O Lord; anoint me with sacred oil of intercession that will baffle enemies and make them surrender and rise no more in the name of Jesus.

31. O Lord, anoint me with sacred oil of war and prayer, that will silence my enemies and make them rise no more in the name of Jesus

32. O Lord, anoint me with sacred oil of prophetic power that will silence my enemies, in the name of Jesus.

33. O Lord, let your hand sustain and make terror in the midst of enemy, let them faint and rise no more in the name of Jesus

34. O Lord, crush the foes after my career and calling, let them rise no more, in the name of Jesus.

35. O Lord, arise, rebuke any power assign to attack my calling, let them fall and rise no more, in the name of Jesus.

36. O Lord, strike down adversaries against my calling, in the name of Jesus.

37. O Lord, speak to me in vision, let me know steps to take, let my enemy weak and rise no more in the name of Jesus.

38. Every marine power assigned to pull me down your time is up, fall down by fire and rise no more, in the name of Jesus.

39. Powers assign to break my covenant with God shall fall and rise no more, in the name of Jesus.

40. Powers praying I should violate the decree of God, so that I may fall, you shall fail, fall and rise no more in the name of Jesus.

41. O Lord, flog my enemies with fire, whip them out of my ministry in the name of Jesus.

42. O Lord, I plead, let your anger end where I went wrong in my ministry and rebuke powers that rise up against me, in the name of Jesus.

43. Powers assign to defile my crown in the dust, your time is up, fall down and rise no more, in the name of Jesus.

44. O Lord, load my heart with wisdom to silence wicked acts of the enemy, let them rise no more, in the name of Jesus.
45. Have mercy and compassion upon me; O my God, let my enemies be in disaster, in the name of Jesus.
46. O Lord, command your angels to guard me in all my ways, let the enemy fall and rise no more, in the name of Jesus.
47. Angels of God; lift me up above my enemies, let them fall and rise no more, in the name of Jesus.
48. Every damaged organ affecting my career; be healed, in the name of Jesus.
49. Powers sponsoring sorrow in my career, fall down and die, and rise no more, in the name of Jesus.
50. Enemies that altar what I said and preach in order to pull me down, your time is up, fall down and rise no more, in the name of Jesus.
51. O Lord, give me strength to keep your commandments and violate the command of Satan, in the name of Jesus.
52. Agents of affliction against my career, fall down and rise no more, in the name of Jesus.

53. Every letter of backwardness prepared for me catch fire and roast to ashes, in the name of Jesus.

54. Career persecutors raised to accuse me, fall down and die, rise no more, in the name of Jesus.

55. Garment of failure organized for me in the spirit, catch fire and burn to ashes in the name of Jesus.

56. My clothing or material placed on evil altar to alter my career, be delivered, work against powers behind it, in the name of Jesus.

57. Witchcraft attack assigned to scatter my career, scatter in the name of Jesus.

58. Thou enemy of my career, what worked for you in the past shall now work against you, in the name of Jesus.

59. Every witchcraft eye monitoring my career, go blind in the name of Jesus.

60. Powers manipulating my career in the spirit, die and rise no more in the name of Jesus.

61. Power that swallowed my career, vomit it now in the name of Jesus.

62. Foundation of failure troubling my career be uprooted in the name of Jesus.

63. Evil parasite assigned to eat my career, die in the name of Jesus.

64. O Lord, let every step enemy take against me lead to greater destruction of their lives in the name of Jesus.

65. My buried potentials come alive, in the name of Jesus.

66. Anointing of excellence come upon me, in the name of Jesus.

67. My hands and feet, receive deliverance from witchcraft bewitchment in the name of Jesus.

68. O Lord, let my dream and vision for my career come to pass in the name of Jesus.

69. O Lord, forgive me don't punish me with your rod, but disgrace my enemy, let them fall and rise no more, in the name of Jesus.

70. O Lord; answer me as the eyes of the slaves look to the hands of their masters, so my eyes look unto you.

71. O Lord, answer me, as the eyes of a maid look to the hands of her mistress, so my eyes look to the Lord.

72. O Lord help me, let my glory shine in the name of Jesus

CHAPTER 6

DEALING WITH ENEMIES OF THE FAMILY

Micah 7:5-6

5. Do not trust a neighbor; put no confidence in a friend. Even with the woman who lies in your embrace guard the words of your lips.

6. For a son dishonors his father, a daughter rises up against her mother, a daughter-in-law against her mother-in-law a man's enemies are the members of his own household.

Psalm 25:1-3

1. In you, LORD my God, I put my trust.

2. I trust in you; do not let me be put to shame, nor let my enemies triumph over me.

3. No one who hopes in you will ever be put to shame, but shame will come on those who are treacherous without cause.

Psalm 91:5-6

5. You will not fear the terror of night, nor the arrow that flies by day,

6. Nor the pestilence that stalks in the darkness, nor the plague that destroys at midday.

PRAYER POINTS

1. I thank you Lord for your protection upon my family, in the name of Jesus.
2. I thank you Lord, that you shall put an end to witchcraft attack, in my family in the name of Jesus.
3. O Lord, extend forgiving spirit unto my family in the name of Jesus.
4. O Lord, show your love to my family, in the name of Jesus.
5. O Lord, cover everyone in my family with blood of Jesus.
6. Blood of Jesus, surround my family against evil arrow, in the name of Jesus.
7. Holy Spirit, illuminate and guide my family in the name of Jesus.
8. Holy Spirit, sanitize my family, in the name of Jesus.
9. My family serves God who determines the number of stars, stars in my family shall rise and shine, while enemies shall fall and rise no more in the name of Jesus.

10. My family serves God who calls us by name for good, enemies are furious, but they shall faint and fall, and rise no more in the name of Jesus.

11. Enemies around me that cunningly rise and conspire against my family, be disgraced forever, in the name of Jesus.

12. Powers that vow my family is confined and cannot escape, shall meet double failure and rise no more, in the name of Jesus.

13. My family; take shelter and rest in the shadow of the Almighty, and let my enemy rise no more, in the name of Jesus.

14. The Lord is the refuge and fortress of my family, any power that rise up against me shall fail and rise no more, in the name of Jesus.

15. Every fowler's snare assign for me break to pieces, catch fire and roast to ashes, let the owner fall down and rise no more in the name of Jesus.

16. Angels of God, guard my family, from striking our feet, against stone of darkness, let our enemies fall and rise no more.

17. O Lord, let my family be at your comfort hand forever, let the enemy that oppose it, be dragged on the floor and rise no more, in the name of Jesus.

18. O Lord, restore my family fortunes, and silence my detractors, in the name of Jesus.
19. Those who boast, let's destroy their family so that their name will be remembered no more, shall fall and rise no more, in the name of Jesus.
20. Those who plot against me and my family, shall scatter and rise no more, in the name of Jesus.
21. Powers that vow my family shall not rejoice in their Maker shall fail woefully, and rise no more in the name of Jesus.
22. O Lord, strike down enemy of my children that vow their youth shall not be sweet, let them fall and rise no more in the name of Jesus.
23. O Lord, strike down enemy that vow my children shall not be pillars of my house at old age, let the enemies fall and rise no more in the name of Jesus.
24. Powers assigned to put my family in captivity shall paralyze and fall, they shall rise no more, in the name of Jesus.
25. Enemies that rise up against me because I serve God who opens hand to satisfy our needs, shall fall and rise no more in the name of Jesus.
26. My family call on God in truth and enemies are against us, they shall fail, and rise no more, in the name of Jesus.

27. My family lives a righteous life, enemies are angry at us, but they shall fall and rise no more in the name of Jesus.

28. My family serves the God that sustains the fatherless and the widow, enemies are unhappy, but they fell and rise no more in the name of Jesus.

29. My family serves the God that frustrates the ways of the wicked.

30. My God blessed the people of my family, enemies are furious, my God silenced them, let them rise no more in the name of Jesus.

31. O Lord, you grant peace to my family, but enemies are angry, strike them, let them rise no more, in the name of Jesus.

32. Torrent assign to sweep my family away dry up, in the name of Jesus.

33. Raging waters assign to sweep my family away, dry up, in the name of Jesus.

34. Children are reward from the Lord, whoever is against my children shall fail and fall, and rise no more, in the name of Jesus.

35. O Lord, preside in my family and let my enemy scatter, and rise no more, in the name of Jesus.

36. My family are all sons and daughters of the Most High, enemies are unhappy, they shall fall and rise no more in Jesus name.

37. O Lord, let those that are against me fall like mere men and women, and rise no more in the name of Jesus.

38. O Lord, do not keep silent, be not be quiet, nor be still, arise strike enemies of my family, let them rise no more, in the name of Jesus.

39. O Lord, strike the heads of enemies that rise against my family, let them fall and rise no more, in the name of Jesus.

40. O Lord, let my family walk with you with blameless heart, in the name of Jesus.

41. Faithless men around my family destined to wipe us away, meet double failure and rise no more, in the name of Jesus.

42. Faithless women around my family assigned to pull us down, your time is up, be put to shame never to rise again.

43. Faithless youths assigned to destroy my family, your time is up, scatter, fall and rise no more, in the name of Jesus.

44. Neighbors with evil intention against my family, scatter and rise no more, in the name of Jesus.

45. Those who slandered my family in secret be silenced forever in the name of Jesus.

46. Whoever have haughty eyes and proud heart to disgrace my family shall rise no more, in the name of Jesus.

47. Those who speak falsely against my family shall not stand before my God, they shall fail, fall and rise no more in the name of Jesus.

48. In family morning prayers, O Lord, silence the wicked in the name of Jesus.

49. O Lord, cut off every evil doer assigned to pollute my family, in the name of Jesus.

50. O Lord, let the days of the wicked vanish like smoke, in the name of Jesus.

51. Enemies against my family; wither like grass and grow no more, in the name of Jesus.

52. Those who use my family name as curse shall be consumed by their curse in the name of Jesus.

53. O Lord; establish my family that no evil wind can pull down, silence my enemy, in the name of Jesus.

54. Any power fighting against my exaltation in my lineage, fall down and rise no more, in the name of Jesus.

55. Those that vow my family shall eat ashes as food shall fail and be ashamed in the name of Jesus.

56. Those who vow my family shall mix our drink with tears shall fail and fade away, in the name of Jesus.

57. In your wrath O Lord, take up my enemies and throw them aside, in the name of Jesus.

58. O Lord, my family give praise to your glory, speak to us today, let our enemy scatter and rise no more, in the name of Jesus.

59. Powers assign to take my family as prisoners, fall down and die, and rise no more, in the name of Jesus.

60. Powers on assignment to break the strength of my family and cause hardship for us, paralyze, fall and rise no more in the name of Jesus.

61. Let the enemies of my family wear out like garment of the old in the name of Jesus.

62. Let those who wish my family to perish fail woefully, but make them perish in the name of Jesus.

63. O Lord, let youths in my family be renewed like the eagles, in the name of Jesus.

64. O Lord, erase iniquities of my family, set us free, in the name of Jesus.

65. O Lord, break and destroy power of darkness on my children's children, in the name of Jesus.

66. O Lord, it is time you clothe my family with splendor and majesty, do it for us now in the name of Jesus.
67. Waters of darkness troubling my family dry up, in the name of Jesus.
68. With honey from the rock my God shall satisfy me, and my enemy shall faint and rise no more, in the name of Jesus.
69. Hear our family prayer O Lord, let our cry of help come unto you, bless us, silence our family in the name of Jesus.
70. O Lord, hold my family together, unify us, establish us, for your kingdom in the name of Jesus.
71. O Lord, show total love for my family forever and ever in the name of Jesus.

CHAPTER 7

DEALING WITH ENEMIES THAT RISE UP AGAINST PROSPERITY

Isaiah 22:22

22. I will place on his shoulder the key to the house of David; what he opens no one can shut, and what he shuts no one can open.

Genesis 12:2-3

2. "I will make you into a great nation, and I will bless you; I will make your name great, and you will be a blessing.

3. I will bless those who bless you, and whoever curses you I will curse; and all peoples on earth will be blessed through you."

Deuteronomy 15:6

6. For the LORD your God will bless you as he has promised, and you will lend to many nations but will borrow from none. You will rule over many nations but none will rule over you.

PRAYER POINTS

THE WICKED SHALL RISE NO MORE

1. I thank my God who will silence enemies that rise up against my prosperity, in the name of Jesus

2. I praise my God; He shall prosper me, in the name of Jesus.

3. O Lord, forgive my sins open doors of prosperity to me, in the name of Jesus.

4. O Lord, let your forgiveness bring joy to my life, in the name of Jesus.

5. Blood of Jesus, cover my wealth, my career and my life in the name of Jesus.

6. I drink blood of Jesus for strength and vitality, in the name of Jesus.

7. Father Lord, incubate me with fire of Holy Ghost, in the name of Jesus.

8. Holy Spirit, guide me through the wilderness of life, in the name of Jesus.

9. Enemy that fights my fortune shall be cut off and shall rise no more, in the name of Jesus.

10. The house the Lord builds for me shall not be pulled down, whoever try to pull it down shall fall and rise no more in Jesus name.

11. O Lord, have mercy upon me, let my prosperity door open, and let my enemy fall and rise no more, in the name of Jesus.

12. O Lord, have hand shake of goodness that promote life to me, let my enemy turn back and leave forever, in the name of Jesus.

13. Dark seas that lifted voice against my prosperity, shut up, and rise no more in the name of Jesus.

14. I serve God who rain supplies of wealth on my life, my enemies are in rage, they fall and shall rise no more in the name of Jesus.

15. O Lord, answer me when I call upon you, let my enemies sleep off; let them rise no more, in the name of Jesus.

16. O Lord, satisfy me by the fruits of my works, put enemies to shame, let them fall and rise no more in the name of Jesus.

17. Every biting demon against my prosperity, lose your teeth, fall down and rise no more, in the name of Jesus.

18. Every wall of darkness raised against my success, I pull you down, you shall rise no more, in the name of Jesus.

19. Witch doctors working against my prosperity paralyze and be helpless, in the name of Jesus.

20. I recover my prosperity in the hands of the dead in the name of Jesus.

21. O Lord, let wealth change hands in my life and favor me, in the name of Jesus.

22. Those who vow my land shall not yield its harvest, fall and rise no more, in the name of Jesus.

23. Those that vow my investment shall not expand will fail and faint as God shall bless me, while my enemies shall collapse and rise no more in the name of Jesus.

24. I serve a Living God who supplies the earth with rain of blessing, I am blessed but my enemies are furious, they shall fall and rise no more in the name of Jesus.

25. When I sow in tears, I shall reap with songs of joy while my enemy shall rise no more, in the name of Jesus.

26. Powers that are angry because my God bring joy and prosperity to my life; shall perish and rise no more in the name of Jesus.

27. Enemy shall not subject me to tribute; they shall fail and rise no more, in the name of Jesus.

28. Marine power assigned to scatter my breakthrough, fall down and rise no more, in the name of Jesus.

29. Every power that vow I will die as a poor person and in shame, you are not my God, fall and rise no more, in the name of Jesus.

30. Every bread of sorrow organized for me in the spirit, I reject you and cast you to lake of fire in the name of Jesus.
31. O Lord, speak wealth to my life, let my enemy count failure and fall, never to rise again, in the name of Jesus.
32. Evil hands collecting my proceeds in the dream; wither in the name of Jesus.
33. Every blockage against my prosperity, expire, let powers behind it, die and rise no more, in the name of Jesus.
34. Every waster assign against my prosperity, expire, let powers behind it, die and rise no more, in the name of Jesus.
35. Every demonic stagnation against my prosperity, expire in the name of Jesus.
36. Every bewitched account I operate be delivered from the grip of darkness and let spirit of God take over, in the name of Jesus.
37. My pocket, purse and bank account shall not leak in the name of Jesus.
38. O Lord; deliver me from anti-prosperity powers, strike them, let them fall and rise no more, in the name of Jesus.
39. O Lord, feed me with information of breakthrough that will make me rejoice and be glad, in the name of Jesus.

40. Every cloud of uncertainty upon my prosperity clear away in the name of Jesus.
41. Every evil hand laid upon my investment, paralyze and wither in the name of Jesus.
42. Every satanic consultation against my prosperity, scatter in the name of Jesus.
43. Powers consulted to wreck my business, paralyze and expire in the name of Jesus.
44. Evil ship carting away my wealth, break down, angels of God, take action and recover my wealth to me, in the name of Jesus.
45. O God arise; waste powers of dark forces working against my prosperity in the name of Jesus.
46. I smash the head of poverty and bury powers behind it in the name of Jesus.
47. Poverty identification number or mark in my body clear away, in the name of Jesus.
48. Every financial hindrance taking my steps backward enough is enough, clear away in the name of Jesus.
49. Inherited poverty troubling my finance expire and rise no more, in the name of Jesus.
50. Every altar of darkness erected to swallow my wealth, catch fire and roast to ashes, in the name of Jesus.

51. O Lord, teach me divine secret of wealth and prosperity in the name of Jesus.

52. Every strange money troubling my wealth, expire in the name of Jesus.

53. O God arise, bring the plan of oppressors against my prosperity to nothing, in the name of Jesus.

54. Satanic intermediary reporting me to satanic kingdom, fall down and rise no more, in the name of Jesus.

55. Every power blocking me from my breakthrough, your time is up, fall down and rise no more, in the name of Jesus.

56. Dark power assigned to pursue me from my garden of prosperity, fall down and rise no more, in the name of Jesus.

57. Every power sitting on my wealth, I recover it from you, and I fling you like piece of paper never to rise again in the name of Jesus.

58. Every arrow of poverty, fired against my prosperity, go back to your sender, in the name of Jesus.

59. Time table of poverty waiting for maturity day, catch fire and roast to ashes, in the name of Jesus.

60. Every curse of financial bondage, break in the name of Jesus.

61. I pursue and overtake my enemies and recover my wealth from them, in the name of Jesus.

62. O Lord, uncover to me the key of my prosperity and doors of breakthrough, in the name of Jesus.

63. O Lord, return my stolen blessing and let my enemies be in disarray, in the name of Jesus.

64. Blessing of the Living God, invade my life, in the name of Jesus.

65. My prosperity, escape from the captivity of the wicked and locate me, in the name of Jesus.

66. By the power of the Living God, I withdraw my blessing from the altar of darkness, in the name of Jesus.

67. By the power of the Living God, I withdraw my breakthrough from altar of darkness and command the evil priest in charge to fall down and rise no more in the name of Jesus.

68. By the power of the Living God, I withdraw my prosperity from the altar of darkness and command the evil priest, in charge to fall down and rise no more, in the name of Jesus.

69. O Lord, let harvest meet harvest in my life, in the name of Jesus.

70. O Lord, network me to divine helpers that will change the story of my life, in the name of Jesus.

71.O Lord, link and lead me to those who will help me and make me prosper, in the name of Jesus.

CHAPTER 8

DEALING WITH ENEMIES THAT RISE UP AGAINST DELIVERANCE AND PEACE

Obadiah 1:17-18

17. But on Mount Zion will be deliverance; it will be holy, and Jacob will possess his inheritance.

18. The house of Jacob will be a fire and the house of Joseph a flame; the house of Esau will be stubble, and they will set it on fire and consume it. There will be no survivors from the house of Esau." The LORD has spoken.

Isaiah 43:2

2. When you pass through the waters, I will be with you; and when you pass through the rivers, they will not sweep over you. When you walk through the fire, you will not be burned; the flames will not set you ablaze.

Exodus 15:9-10

9. The enemy boasted, 'I will pursue, I will overtake them. I will divide the spoils; I will gorge myself on them. I will draw my sword and my hand will destroy them.'

10. But you blew with your breath, and the sea covered them. They sank like lead in the mighty waters.

PRAYER POINTS

1. I thank you Lord for drawing me to my place of deliverance and peace in the name of Jesus.
2. I thank you Lord for spiritual gifts upon my life, in the name of Jesus.
3. O Lord; forgive me the sins I commit so as to get full deliverance, in the name of Jesus.
4. Lord Jesus, lay your hand of forgiveness upon my life in the name of Jesus.
5. Blood of Jesus, cleanse me and make me whole, in the name of Jesus.
6. I drink blood of Jesus, to purify me and deliver me of impurity in my body in the name of Jesus.
7. Holy Spirit, show me where I have fallen, teach me to rise again, in the name of Jesus.
8. Holy Spirit, arise and be my strength, in the name of Jesus.
9. Holy Ghost, quicken me to prosperity and peace, in the name of Jesus.

10. When my God upholds me when I fall, enemies were bitter, they shall fall and rise no more, in the name of Jesus.

11. O Lord, deliver me from the hand of those who don't know peace, I am for peace, strike them and let them rise no more in the name of Jesus.

12. The Lord will keep me from harm, whoever contests it shall fail and fall, in the name of Jesus.

13. Walls of darkness that surround my enemies as protection, break to pieces and let them be dragged on the floor, in the name of Jesus.

14. My father and my God answer me from thunder cloud and let my enemies fall and rise no more, in the name of Jesus.

15. I open my mouth O Lord, fill it with prayer of deliverance, and let my enemy fall and rise no more, in the name of Jesus.

16. The Lord shall watch over my coming in and my going out without molestation, any power that contests it shall fail and fall never to rise in the name of Jesus.

17. O Lord my God, draw my ears unto you, I am your child, let enemies be confuse and rise no more, in the name of Jesus.

18. O Lord, I come to you, subdue my enemies, let them rise no more, in the name of Jesus.

19. I am like Mount Zion who trust in the Lord, whoever attack me shall paralyze and rise no more in the name of Jesus.
20. The Lord watches over me, whosoever is against me shall be strike and not wake in the name of Jesus.
21. The Lord is my shade at his right hand, whoever dispute it shall fall and fail, never to rise, in the name of Jesus.
22. The sun will not harm me by day, nor the moon by night, whoever contests it shall fall and never rise again in the name of Jesus.
23. O Lord, deliver me from enemies whose mouth are full of lies, put them to shame, fall and rise no more, in the name of Jesus.
24. O Lord, sent forth lightning and scatter my enemies, let them fall and rise no more, in the name of Jesus.
25. My enemies saw I bow down in prayer in holy temple of God, they fall and collapse and rise no more, in the name of Jesus.
26. My God delivered me of flooding my bed with tears, enemies witnessed it and fail, they shall rise no more, in Jesus name.
27. My God heard my cry for mercy and accepts my prayer, enemies panicked and fall, they shall rise no more, in Jesus name.

28. My God trained my hands for war and my fingers for battle, enemies knew this, they fled and fall, they shall rise no more in the name of Jesus.

29. O Lord, be my stronghold and my deliverer, let my enemy fall and rise no more, in the name of Jesus.

30. O Lord, I put my hope on your unfailing love to mankind, but enemies arise and kick against it, let them fall and rise no more in the name of Jesus.

31. O Lord, you grant peace to my life, enemies rise against it, strike them, let them rise no more in the name of Jesus.

32. Those who are for war while I am for peace that rise up against me, O Lord, silence them and let them rise no more in the name of Jesus.

33. Powers that are against me as I lift up my eyes to the hills, be strike by Holy Ghost power, and rise no more, in the name of Jesus.

34. Powers that attack me because I serve God who watches over me do not slumber, shall fail and fall never to rise in the name of Jesus

35. As the mountains surround Jerusalem, so the Lord surround me; any power that attack me shall fall and rise no more in the name of Jesus.

36. Do good to me O Lord, clear away powers that wants me to do evil, let them fall and rise no more, in the name of Jesus.

37. O Lord, turn my hands against my foes let them scatter in the name of Jesus.

38. O Lord, let the punishment of enemy last forever, never to rise up against me, in the name of Jesus.

39. My heart and my flesh, cry out to God, I am answered, my enemies fled, fall flat and rise no more, in the name of Jesus.

40. I lift up my soul for deliverance and forgiveness, let those against it, perish and rise no more, in the name of Jesus.

41. Those who want me to die in trouble, shall fail, fall and rise no more, in the name of Jesus.

42. My God who saves me day and night is my Saviour, my enemy know it and fainted, they shall perish and rise no more, in the name of Jesus.

43. O Lord; remove the troubles in my soul, deliver me from the wicked ones, let my enemy perish and rise no more, in the name of Jesus.

44. I break through the walls of enemy and reduce their strongholds to ruin; never shall they rise again, in the name of Jesus.

45. O Lord, plunder every enemy of my soul, let them fail and fall and rise no more, in the name of Jesus.

46. O Lord, deliver me from the hand of the wicked, let them perish and rise no more in the name of Jesus.

47. My Father and my God that wraps himself in light as with a garment, wrap my destiny with garment of deliverance, let my enemies scatter in the name of Jesus.

48. O Lord, deliver me, don't hide your face from me, in the name of Jesus.

49. O Lord, build your hedge of fire around me, and let my enemy surrender, in the name of Jesus.

50. Every stubborn pursuer of my life, your time is up, summersault and die, in the name of Jesus.

51. Every wall of challenge raised against my deliverance, I pull you down in the name of Jesus.

52. Thou gate of death waiting to welcome me to your house, catch fire and roast to ashes, in the name of Jesus.

53. Stronghold of darkness assign to collect my prayer and render me useless, I pull you down, in the name of Jesus.

54.My father in heaven that stretches out the heavens like a tenth, let me dwell in your tenth of power and deliverance, let my enemies fall and rise no more in the name of Jesus.

55.O Lord, set boundary around me, enemies cannot cross, let them be consumed with their evil intention, in the name of Jesus.

56.Candle of the wicked lighted to pull me down, quench and be roasted to ashes, in the name of Jesus.

57.Plagues of darkness around me scatter, in the name of Jesus.

58.God that makes flames of fire his servants, let flames of fire devour works of darkness after my destiny in the name of Jesus.

59.O Lord, at the sound of your thunder let enemy scatter and rise no more, in the name of Jesus.

60.O Lord, rebuke marine powers that vow I will not make it in life, set them apart for destruction, in the name of Jesus.

61.My star, arise and shine in the name of Jesus.

62.My Father and my God that ride on the wings of the wind use your power to deliver me to ride with you, in the name of Jesus.

63.Powers that vow I will not make it in life, go down to bottomless pit and rise no more, in the name of Jesus.

64. O Lord, quench my thirst, deliver me from poverty and famine of life, in the name of Jesus.

65. Every cage assigned to imprison my destiny, catch fire and roast to ashes, in the name of Jesus.

66. Yoke of poverty, designed for me, break in the name of Jesus.

67. My God, that makes wind his messenger, send message of deliverance and success to my life, and let my enemies fall and rise no more.

68. I reject destiny burial and claim destiny prosperity in the name of Jesus.

69. Effects of evil hands laid on me, backfire and destroy power behind it in the name of Jesus.

70. O Lord, rub me with heavenly oil that will make my face shine, in the name of Jesus.

71. O Lord, feed me with heavenly wine that gladdens the heart, in the name of Jesus.

72. O Lord, put songs of victory in my mouth to the glory of deliverance you establish in my life, in the name of Jesus.

CHAPTER 9

DEALING WITH ENEMIES AGAINST MY JOY

Lamentation 5:7-9

7. Our fathers sinned and are no more, and we bear their punishment.

8. Slaves rule over us, and there is none to free us from their hands.

9. We get our bread at the risk of our lives because of the sword in the desert.

Joel 2:23-24

23. Be glad, O people of Zion, rejoice in the LORD your God, for he has given you the autumn rains in righteousness. He sends you abundant showers, both autumn and spring rains, as before.

24. The threshing floors will be filled with grain; the vats will overflow with new wine and oil.

Psalm 1:3

3. That person is like a tree planted by streams of water, which yields its fruit in season and whose leaf does not wither whatever he does prospers.

PRAYER POINTS

1. I thank my God for lifting me out of pit of sorrow, and put me in palace of joy, in the name of Jesus.
2. I thank you Lord for your wonderful love, in the name of Jesus.
3. O Lord, forgive me, let me be joyful in your presence, in the name of Jesus.
4. Lord Jesus, forgive me every sin blocking my hope and joy, in the name of Jesus.
5. I am cleansed with blood of Jesus to promote joy in my life, in the name of Jesus.
6. I drink blood of Jesus to make me shine and be purified, in the name of Jesus.
7. Holy Spirit, help me to see what is wrong in my life, in the name of Jesus.
8. Holy Spirit, visit me with hands of majesty, in the name of Jesus.
9. Holy Spirit, transform my life, make me great in the name of Jesus.
10. My joy is full, as my God reach down his hands from heaven and rescue me, enemies were shocked, they fall and rise no more.

11. I sing a new song to my Lord, enemies were in awe they fell and shall not rise, in the name of Jesus.

12. Those that don't want me to praise my God forever and ever shall fall and rise no more, in the name of Jesus.

13. Since I speak of the glorious splendor of the Lord, enemies are against me, they shall fail and fall and rise no more in the name of Jesus.

14. As I celebrate abundant goodness of God, enemies that rise up to challenge me shall fall and rise no more, in Jesus name.

15. Enemies who rise up against me because I serve God whose kingdom is an everlasting kingdom, shall fall and rise no more in the name of Jesus.

16. Powers that attacked me because I serve God whose dominion endures through all generations, shall fall and rise no more in the name of Jesus.

17. Because I serve my God who give me my food at proper time, and enemy rise against me, the enemy shall fall and rise no more in the name of Jesus.

18. When enemies see how pleasant and fitting I praise God, they arise and attack me, but my God defends me, they fell and rise no more in the name of Jesus.

19. I praise God, who builds up Jerusalem, enemies are furious at me, they fell and rise no more, in the name of Jesus.

20. I serve God who gathered the exiles of Israel and put smiles in their face, enemies attack me, but they fell and rise no more in the name of Jesus.

21. I sing to the Lord with thanksgiving, but enemies are unhappy, O God strike them, let them fall and rise no more, in Jesus name.

22. I make music to my God in harp, but enemies are furious at me, O God strike them, let them fall and rise no more in the name of Jesus.

23. I serve my God who supplies rain of joy unto me, but enemies kick against it, they fall and rise no more in the name of Jesus.

24. I praise my God in heavens, enemies are angry because they praise other gods, they rise to attack me, my God silenced them, in the name of Jesus.

25. I praise my God along with heavenly angels, enemies are angry, my God strike them, let them rise no more, in the name of Jesus.

26. I praise my God along with heavenly hosts, enemies are furious at me, but my God rebuked them, they fell and rise no more in the name of Jesus.

27. I praise my God who commanded and everything were created, enemies ran mad of this, but God strike them, they fell and rise no more in the name of Jesus.

28. Powers assigned to disallow me to praise God for his acts of power, I strike you down, you shall arise no more, in the name of Jesus.

29. Those against me for praising God in his surpassing greatness receive Holy Ghost slap, fall down and rise no more, in Jesus name.

30. Power in the spirit assign to highjack trumpet sound in my mouth, fall down and rise no more, in the name of Jesus.

31. Praise be to God, who do not allow enemies tear me with their teeth, they fell and rise no more, in the name of Jesus.

32. Hallelujah, I escaped like a bird out of the fowler's snare, in the name of Jesus.

33. Hallelujah, the snare of the enemy is broken, I escaped, my enemy fall and rise no more, in the name of Jesus.

34. My mouth is filled with laughter, enemies that are against me are cut off and rise no more, in the name of Jesus.

35. My tongue sing songs of joy, every enemy against it shall be cut off, never shall they rise again, in the name of Jesus.

36. Powers blocking me to exalt my God the King of kings, shut up, fall down and rise no more in the name of Jesus.

37. Every power with evil padlock assign to padlock my mouth in the spirit, so that I may not praise my God on daily basis, fall down and rise no more in the name of Jesus.

38. Any power on assignment to padlock my mouth, not to share testimony, paralyze, fall down and rise no more in the name of Jesus.

39. I will celebrate God's abundant goodness upon my family, whoever is against it, I silence you to deep sleep, in the name of Jesus.

40. I praise my God with all my heart, enemies are unhappy, they fainted and rise no more, in the name of Jesus.

41. I praise my God whose anger is no more over my life, I am happy my enemies fainted, they fell and rise no more in the name of Jesus.

42. My God fed me with bread of life, while my enemies ate bread of tears, they fell and rise no more in the name of Jesus.

43. Let plantations of God germinate in my home for signs and wonders, let enemies see it and faint, never shall they wake again in the name of Jesus.

44. Angels of God arise for my sake, begin the music, strike the tambourine, let me dance, and let my enemies be silenced forever in the name of Jesus.

45. O God, remove burden from my shoulder, I burst to laughter, enemies see it, they were shocked, fall and rise no more in the name of Jesus.

46. Those that vow I will not dwell in the lovely place of God, you are a liar, fall down and rise no more, in the name of Jesus.

47. Every court of darkness raised to judge me, shall catch fire and be raised to the ground, in the name of Jesus.

48. I am blessed because I dwell in the house of the Lord, in the name of Jesus.

49. I am blessed and happy, the Lord is my strength, in the name of Jesus.

50. Powers that are against me to experience happiness, you are not my God, fall down and rise no more, in the name of Jesus.

51. With my mouth I will make my God's fruitfulness known through all generations, enemies shall hear of it and surrender, in the name of Jesus.

52. O Lord, establish my generation in faithfulness to you forever and let enemies be put to shame, never to rise again.

53. Wonders and testimonies of the Lord abound in my life, enemies saw it and were dumbfounded, they fall and rise no more in the name of Jesus.

54. When the surging seas rise up against me, my God still them, enemies see it and fainted, they rise no more in the name of Jesus.

55. With mighty hands, my God scattered my enemies, they fell and rise no more, in the name of Jesus.

56. O Lord, put to shame enemies that are not happy I walk in the light of your presence, let them fall and rise no more in the name of Jesus.

57. Enemies shall not rejoice over me, I shall rejoice over them, they shall fall and rise no more, in the name of Jesus.

58. O Lord, make me glad and happy in my sojourn on earth in the name of Jesus.

59. In my years on earth I will not die in trouble in the name of Jesus.

60. O Lord, let your favor rest upon me, in the name of Jesus.

61. I will proclaim the love of God in the morning and faithfulness at night, whoever is against it shall fail and rise no more in the name of Jesus.

62. I will sing for joy at the works of God upon my life, my enemies are baffled, they fell and rise no more in the name of Jesus.

63. I will flourish like the palm tree and be great, my enemies shall fall and rise no more, in the name of Jesus.

64. I will bear fruit, even at old age and shall excel forever, in the name of Jesus.

65. There shall be no wickedness in me, joy shall fill my heart in the name of Jesus.

66. My God exalted my horn like that of a wild ox, I rout my enemy away, they scatter and rise no more, in the name of Jesus.

67. O Lord, put robe of majesty on me, put everlasting laughter in my mouth, in the name of Jesus.

68. I am a winner, my God makes me mightier than the breakers of the seas, I shall the end of stubborn pursuers after me in the name of Jesus.

69. I am a winner, my God makes me mightier than thunder of the great waters, and my enemies disappear in the name of Jesus.

70. I am a winner, my eyes shall see the defeat of my adversaries, they shall rise no more, in the name of Jesus.

71. O Lord, I thank for your favor upon me, in the name of Jesus.

72. O Lord, I thank you as my enemies perish and rise no more, in the name of Jesus.

YOU HAVE BATTLES TO WIN
TRY THESE BOOKS

1. COMMAND THE DAY: DAILY PRAYER BOOK

Each day of the week is loaded with meanings and divine assurance. God did not create each day of the week for the fun of it. Blessings, success, gifts, resources, hopes, portfolios, duties, rights, prophecies, warnings and challenges, are loaded in each day.

Do you know the language, command or decree you can use to claim what belongs to you in each day of the week? Do you know in Christendom, Monday can be equated to one of the days of creation in Genesis chapter one? Do you know creation lasted for six days and God rested on the seventh day? What day of the week can Christian equate as the first day of the week, if we follow Christian calendar? What day can we call day seven?

This book shall give insight to these questions. It shall explain how you can command each day of the week according to creation in the book of Genesis chapter one.

Above all, you shall exercise your right and claim what is hidden in each day of the week.
Check for this in <u>**COMMAND THE DAY: DAILY PRAYER BOOK**</u>

2. <u>PRAYER TO REMEMBER DREAMS</u>

A lot of people are passing through this spiritual epidemic on a daily basis. Their dream life is epileptic, having no ability to remember all dreams they dream, or sometimes forget everything entirely. This is nothing but spiritual havoc you need to erase from your spiritual record.
The answer to every form of spiritual blackout caused by spiritual erasers is found in, <u>**PRAYER TO REMEMBER DREAMS**</u>

3. <u>100% CONFESSIONS AND PROPHECIES TO LOCATE HELPERS AND HELPERS TO LOCATE YOU</u>

This is a wonderful book on confessions and prophecies to locate helpers and helpers to locate you. It is a prayer book loaded with over two thousand (2,000) prayer points.

The book unravels how to locate unknown helpers, prayers to arrest mind of helpers and prayers for manifestation after encounter with helpers.

4. ANOINTING FOR ELEVENTH HOUR HELP: HOPE AND HELP FOR YOUR TURBULENT TIMES

This book tells much of what to do at injury hour called eleventh hour. When you read and use this book as prescribed fear shall vanish in your life when pursuing a project, career or contract.

5. PRAYER TO LOCATE HELPERS AND HELPERS TO LOCATE YOU

Our divine helper is God. He created us to be together and be of help to one another. In the midst of no help we lost out, ending our journey in the wilderness.

There are keys assign to open right doors of life. You need right key to locate your helpers. Enough is enough; of suffering in silence.

With this book, you shall locate your helpers while your helpers shall locate you.

6. <u>FIRE FOR FIRE PART ONE: (PRAYER BOOK BOOK 1)</u>

This prayer book is fast at answering spiritual problems. It is a bulldozer prayer book, full of prayers all through. It is highly recommended for night vigil. Testimonies are pouring in daily from users of this book across the world!

7. <u>PRAYER FOR FRUIT OF THE WOMB: EXPECTING MOTHERS</u>

This prayer book is children magnet. By faith and believe in God Almighty, as soon as you use this book open doors to child bearing shall be yours. Amen

8. <u>PRAYER FOR PREGNANT WOMEN: WITH ALL CHRISTIAN NAMES AND MEANINGS</u>

This is a spiritual prayer book loaded with prayers of solution for pregnant women. As soon as you take in, the prayers you shall pray from day one of conception to the day of delivery are written in this book.

9. <u>**WARFARE IN THE OFFICE: PRAYER TO SILENCE TOUGH TIMES IN OFFICE**</u>

It is high time you pray prayers of power must change hands in office. Use this book and liberate yourself from every form of office yoke.

10. <u>**MY MARRIAGE SHALL NOT BREAK: THE SECRET TO LOVE AND MARRIAGE THAT LASTS**</u>

Marriage is corner piece of life, happiness and joy. You need to hold it tight and guide it from wicked intruders and destroyer of homes.

11. <u>**VICTORY OVER SATANIC HOUSE PART ONE: RIDDING YOUR HOME OF SPIRITUAL DARKNESS**</u>

Are you a tenant, Land lord bombarded left and right, front and back by wicked people around you?
With this book you shall be liberated from the hooks of the enemy.

12. <u>**DICTIONARY OF DREAMS: THE DREAM INTERPRETATION**</u>

<u>DICTIONARY WITH SYMBOLS, SIGNS, AND MEANINGS</u>

This is a must book for every home. It gives accurate details to about **10,000 (Ten thousand) dreams and interpretations,** written in alphabetical order for quick reference and easy digestion. The book portrays spiritual revelations with sound prophetic guidelines. It is loaded with Biblical references and violent prayers.
Ask for yours today.

For Further Enquiries Contact
THE AUTHOR
EVANGELIST TELLA OLAYERI
P.O. Box 1872 Shomolu Lagos.
Tel: 08023583168

FROM AUTHOR'S DESK

BEFORE YOU GO

Hello,

Thank you for purchasing this book. Would you consider posting a review about this book? In addition to providing feedback and arousing others into Christ's bosom, reviews can help other customers to know about the book.

Please take a minute to leave a review on this book.

I would appreciate that!

Thank you in advance, for your review and your patronage!!

Feel free to drop us your prayer request. We will join faith with you and God's power will be released in your life and issue in question.

http://tellaolayeri.com/prayerrequest.php

NOTE: You can get all my books from my website http://tellaolayeri.com

GOOD NEWS!!!

My audiobook is now available, to get one visit **acx.com** and search **"Tella Olayeri."**

Brethren, to be loaded and reloaded visit: amazon.com/author/tellaolayeri for a full spiritual sojourn for my books.

Thanks.